Mohabbat, Khat and you

Kunal Agarwal

Ukiyoto Publishing

All global publishing rights are held by

Ukiyoto Publishing

Published in 2023

Content Copyright © Kunal Agarwal
ISBN 9789359200620

All rights reserved.
No part of this publication may be reproduced,
transmitted, or stored in a retrieval system, in any
form by any means, electronic, mechanical,
photocopying, recording or otherwise, without the
prior permission of the publisher.

The moral rights of the author have been asserted.

This is a work of fiction. Names, characters, businesses,
places, events, locales, and incidents are either the
products of the author's imagination or used in a
fictitious manner. Any resemblance to actual persons,
living or dead, or actual events is purely coincidental.

This book is sold subject to the condition that it shall
not by way of trade or otherwise, be lent, resold, hired
out or otherwise circulated, without the publisher's
prior consent, in any form of binding or cover other
than that in which it is published.

*In the memory of my mother
Surekha Agarwal*

Acknowledgements

There may be only one name listed as the writer of this book, but this book wouldn't have been possible without the support and encouragement of the following people: My father, Jitender Agarwal, always had an optimistic attitude towards me and guided me in every stage of my life. Thank you *Papa*!

My brother, Kaushik Agarwal, helped me finish this book. Thank you *Bhaiya*!

I would also like to extend my gratitude to Om Prakash Agarwal and Santosh Agarwal, who are no less than my parents. Thank you, *Bade Papa* and *Badi Mummy*, for always being there for us!

Special thanks to Atul Agarwal, Sandeep Agarwal and Alok Agarwal you guys are a huge part of this accomplishment.

My beautiful sisters, Neha Sai Charan Singh, Neelam Harshit Gangal, Apeksha Agarwal and Natasha Ajay Reddy, Thank you for the constant love and support.

I will always be indebted to Late Puranmal Agarwal, Late Radhabai Agarwal, Late Jai Narayan Agarwal and Savitri Devi Agarwal for all the blessings.

A special heartfelt thank you to Fatima for convincing me to write this book.

And to all my friends and family who have been an important part of my life.

Preface

In the realm of literature, poetry holds a unique place. It is a symphony of words that transcends the boundaries of language and culture, touching the deepest recesses of the human soul. With Poetry, there is a certain kind of magic that comes alive when emotions are woven into words and "Mohabbat Khat and You" is a genuine attempt to extend these boundaries.

It is an exquisite collection of poetry that delves into the depths of the heart, offering readers a breathtaking roller coaster ride of emotions through the lens of a first-time writer. The verses in this book dance seamlessly between Hindi and English, crafting a vivid tapestry of sentiments that resonate with the human experience.

As you embark on this literary journey, you will encounter countless emotions and feelings of love, passion, longing, and heartbreak. Each poem is a portal into the author's soul. It serves as a reminder that emotions, no matter how intense or delicate, are a universal thread that binds us all.

Ek naye din ki shuruwat, ek naya aagaaz laya hun,
Tu padhte rahe khud ko main tere liye ek nayi kavita laya hun.

How can this be true?

How can nature allow this?

How can God, the almighty forces, be so careless in this regard?

How can someone mean the world to me and I don't even mean a grain to them?

Tumhe humare jaisa aur koi kaha milega?

Tumhe phool toh kayi lakar denge, tumhe sara bagicha kaun laakar dega?

Why do you smoke so much?

- For Love.

For Love?

- So that one day I'll be able to quit for my love.

Why don't you quit now?

- Then what purpose would my love serve?

But it's killing you.

- Yes, it is.

What if you don't find love?

- Well then, I am glad that I don't have to live in a world without love for long.

Jab jab pata puchta hun tumhara un taaron se woh rooth jatey hai,

Khabar aayi hai unhe ki aap hi ki khwahishon pe woh toot jatey hai.

Metaphor

I have been loved before. By different people in different ways. Not in the ways I prefer, but they loved regardless. I don't blame them. The concept of love for them and me is different. They stayed because they loved me and the love wanted me to stay for them.

Like trying to find their essence in the poems that I write about myself.

Like the love found at the end of a cigarette butt.

Like a child being forced to eat.

Like a dream that had just woken up.

Like the dark clouds writing the sun.

Like a writer stuck on this poem.

Like a poem writing its author.

Like mistakes trying to find love.

Like a hole in the heart.

Like an unfinished tragedy.

Like a voice trying to find a war cry.

Like all the other metaphors that don't really make sense, I have been loved.

I met a girl at the airport last week.

Today, I realized I am in love and 24 years of all wrong metaphors

Ek umr kam padhjati hai logoh ko janneh mein pehchanney mein,

Ek umr kam padhjati hai aapke sath waqt beetane mein.

In an alternate universe where paper maps are made of magic, where it would ask where do you want to go?

I would say, "Take me to her."

Jeeney ke kitne din hai yeh gin kar kya karoge?

Guzrey huey lamho mein kabhi hamey bhi yaad karoge?

10   Mohabbat, Khat and you

And that's the thing about you,

You are a wildflower and you are better left to the wild.

I cannot bring you home and nurture you with tamed love.

You were born so forests could grow inside you.

Neend toh haram hai, usi ki baaton ka khayal hai.
Ye raat uski baaton mein kat jayegi,
Subah uska naam lekar kahi gum hojayegi

I'll name us time, because not today but we were meant to meet in eternity.

I'll name us time, because once lost, we'll never find each other.

I'll name us time, because that is what brought us together.

I'll name us time, because you heal me and I heal you.

I'll name us time, because it reminds us of the past, the memories we build in the present and the dreams we dreamt of the future.

I'll name us time, because that's the only thing we can give each other.

I'll name us time, because we are running out of it.

I'll name us time, because what we have is equally precious.

I'll name us time, because neither of us is enough for either of us.

I'll name us time because, that's the only thing that lasts forever.

Suna hai har guldastey par kisi ka naam likha hota hai,
Par aapko dekh kar lagta hai ki duniya bhar key bagichey bhi kam padh jayengey.

In front of people, I pretend love is cheap. I tell them it's something hippies do. I tell my dad that love is not my cup of tea. In front of my friends, I tell them love is something found in cigarette shops. But at night, when I visit a restaurant, I know I will lick a single drop of love from a leftover spoon. I would go beg for it in nightclubs, restaurants, hospitals and airports. But that's the thing about people who beg: they don't get it in the right places and don't deserve it in the wrong places.

Woh mujhse zyada mere jaisi hai toh
Main use mujhse zyada kyu na chahun?

There are too many mediocre things in life. Make sure love isn't one of them.

Uske hasne par humne hasna band kardiya tha,

Par uske rone par humare marne ki aadat abhi gayi nahi.

There is someone out there I know who will love me for who I exactly am: my flaws, my ideologies and my love, but today I write the saddest stories of all. The person I seek, seeks me too and yet neither of us knows about each other's existence.

Instagram aur messaging ke zamane mein aap mere khat padhne aa gaye.

Ye kaisa gunah kar rahe ho, aap humse mohabbat karne aa gaye.

Have you ever heard of heartbroken syndrome?

Yes, I did, but I never encountered a case of such a manner

You are looking at one right now!

It's very rare for a heartbreak to kill you.

I am one of those.

"Those who die when they love."

Woh jinhe mere lafz par aitbaar tha
Woh jinhe meri khamoshi se bhi pyaar tha
Aaj dhundte honge khud ko kisi aur kitaab mein,
woh jinhey maine apni har kitaab mein likha tha.

How do they live?

The ones who weren't loved back?

The ones who never learned to survive on empty plates?

How are they capable of bearing their own hearts?

Mujhe apni kahani aur likhni hai tum saath kagaz palatne ka wada toh karoh

Mujhe hazar khwaishen hai tumsey rooth janey ki tum ek bar manane ka wada toh karo

Mujhe un raston par aur chalna hai tum manzil par milne ka wada toh karo

Mujhe humare bitaye huey waqt ka hisab karna hai tum bewaqt milna shuru toh karo.

I think I should throw away my books of love. I have not learned it right. Something went wrong. I should have never started writing poems on love. I should stop with my writings and readings too, because it's simple: whatever I learned, I loved the same way and for whatever I have loved, I have not been loved back.

The way you do it.
The way you hold my hands.
The way you kiss my forehead.
The way your hands glide through my hair.
Come, teach me a gentler way to look at myself.
Come, teach me how to love the way you do!

I didn't know myself before you and I don't think I will forget who I am after you.

The only tragedy with this is you are all over the place and I am nowhere near you.

God was never kind to himself; I think he needs my help.

"God convinced us that love is found in the dark until I realized God lives there too!"

The moon reads her stories and tucks her by her side.

The cupids have sent her so many letters that she lost her own address.

End of the world resides on her lips.

No one has come alive out of it, Not even me.

Maine bahut likha hai, Maine tujhe likha hai.
Tere saath mohabbat likha hai.
Tujhse lad kar bhi,
Tujhse bichad kar bhi,
Tujhe maine apne pas likha hai.

Woh hateli dikhti kaisi hogi jisme naam uska likha ho,

Woh haath dikhta kaisa hoga jise thaamta uska haath ho,

Woh jo bhul jaati hai zulf sawarna, woh ayiney ko dekhta kon hai jisme ehsaas uska na ho,

Woh jo kuch raaz chupa kar chalti hai, sunta kon hai bewafai uski.

Suno....?

Khwahishein hum puri na kar sake tumhare pyaar mein toot kar,

Unhe sambhal kar rakhna kuch din,

Taare tumse abhi pyaar karna seekh rahe hai.

I write this to you hoping to meet you someday in a museum full of love and war.

We are museums.

The walls made of tragedies and ceilings of history.

They are mostly empty, but I decorated them with every artifact that reminds me of you.

Swordsmen have defined our love over spilled blood and daggers have stories knitted onto them.

The gun barrels have meddled with the fear of bullets and bullets have loved our hearts like no other.

Bows and arrows were never meant to be together.

I hold the power of canons in my heart and you hold fire in your touch.

There are artworks painted with grief all over them.

Anything that ever existed between us was at war but never at peace, never in love.

Love and history have never been kind to each other; one has a taste for blood and the other for tragedies.

Maybe I have loved you with shields and armor and that is why all I ever received was spears and lances.

And in a billion years, when life is still intact on earth, when our bodies have been pushed deep beneath the surface, we shall meet as souls.

I wish to be born this time as a hummingbird after numerous failed attempts of being born as mammals, insects, or reptiles for the petty sins I have committed. I have always loved the bright gorget of the hummingbirds and I know you like plants, so I pray you become a plant of any kind you wish to.

I will find you like I always have in all those reincarnated births where we have failed to love each other. I will find you this time because your flowers have those bright colours that attract my eyes. I will rob your nectar like I have always robbed your heart, but this time, you will be willing to give it to me.

We will be dependent on each other, we will be the reason for co-evolution of each other, and we will still be in love with each other but the only difference is, this time, we won't let our differences kill each other, but rather we make them our reason to live with each other.

This is the kind of love that goes unnoticed around the world, a love that's not possible for humans to comprehend. So, I wish I was not born as a human to love you the way plants and birds do.

Ek din tumhare hisse me zarur aaunga.

Tumhare dil me jagah banane ki unn koshisho me zarur aaunga.

Shayad tumhare pyaar me na sahi par tumhare khayalon me zarur aaunga.

Shayad tumhare zikr me na sahi par tumhari aadaton me zarur aaunga.

Woh sab dohraunga, tumhari kahani me shabd banke, main phir aaunga.

Tumhare haaton ki lakeeron me apna naam padhney main phir aaunga.

Tumhari khwaishon me unn khwabon ko pura karne main zarur aunga.

Qayamat ke din tumhara faisla banke main haar jaunga.

Tumhare ikraar me na sahi tumhare inkaar me zarur aaunga.

Aaunga main lekar woh sare wadein phir todney ke liye.

Main phir aaunga tumse pyaar karne, tumse aitbaar karne, tumse haar jane, khud se jeet jane aur unn sabhi bematlab baaton ko sach karne.

Ek din main zarur aaunga.

Tumse khud ka woh hisssa mangne.

Tumhe apna banane ki koshish me.

Tumhare woh sarey khat padhne.

Tumhari aankhon me apna ghar basane. Main aaunga.

Phool tutne par awaaz kaha karta hai?

Tu mere saath raha kar mujhe acha lagta hai.

Door se tujhe jo dekhta hoon, sab kuch uljha dikhta hai,

Paas jo tere aaun, tere siva aur kuch kaha dikhta hai.

Nafrat hai mujhe tumse aur tumhari kahaniyon se.
Har panne par fareb likha hai apne.
Har kitaab me zaalim kiya hai hume.
Nafrat hai mujhe tumse aur tumhari aadaton se.
Yuhi kisi ke bhi gale lag gaye par baat jab humari aayi,
Humari khushboo ko bhi apnane se inkaar kardiya.

Pata nahi kab logon me wafa dhundte dhunte humne ye zehar pee liya,

Lagta hai yeh toh zehar ki bhi bewafai thi jisne hume marne bhi na diya.

Ek ladki thi bholi bhali si
Kitaabon se woh darti thi.

Pyaar me woh behosh rehti thi.

Apni hi duniya me madhosh rehti thi, kisi bhi kone me ro diya karti thi.

Ab hum usse sawarte ya muskurate,

Bas aisi humari sapno ki raani thi.

Faraq sirf itna tha ki woh haqeeqat se wakif nahi thi kyuki woh hamare kitabon ke panno ki ek kahani thi.

Woh humare takiye pe padi ek khwab thi jo har roj neendo me aati thi

Uski maujudgi ka wajood humari syahi deti thi, uski dhadkan bhi toh humari hi kalakari thi.

Bas bholi bhali si ek ladki thi.

Pyaar se woh darti thi.

Tum uss mausam ki tarah ho jo pal bhar me badal jati ho.

Tum uss baarish ki tarah ho jo yuhi baras jaati ho.

Mera kya, main toh bas ek chaata hun, jab tu hoti hai tabhi logon ko yaad aata hun.

Tera aur mera rishta bhi bada atrangi hai main paida bhi hua toh tujhme bheegne ke liye,

Tum jo mujhe chu kar guzar gayi, haal-e -dil zindagi muqammal ho gayi.

Aaj samandar ke unn labon pe suraj dhal gaya hai, lagta hai tere chehre ki hasi dekh aasman bhi jhuk gaaya hai.

Uss door aandhi me koi tujhe pukar raha hai tere pairon tale zameen bhi tujhe aaj bula rahi hai.

Ye lehre tujhme bheegna chahti hai.

Ye reth tujhe apna banana chahti hai.

Inn hawaon ko teri zulfon se mohabatt hogayi hai.

Inn ghataon ko teri nazdikiyon ki aadat si hogayi hai.

Uss sagar ki gehrayi me teri kahaniyan jhalakti hai, teri aankhon ki nami me bhi toh woh aandhi barasti hai.

Mere alfaaz aaj teri aankhon se kuch aur der nazrein milana chahte hai,

Tere labon pe kuch aur der teherna chahte hai, teri khushbu se kuch aur der guftagu karna chahte hai.

Aaj mera pyar iss kagaz par ek kavita sa utar gaya hai, par kyu kaid karu tujhe iss kagaz me, tu inn lakiro ki bandish se azad hi achi lagti hai.

Tu in lehron ki karvaton se azad hi achi lagti hai.

Tu....bas tu achi lagti hai.

The first poem.

My bones they pour a love of no kind. All it goes is in vain. Not the one that runs blood, the one that doesn't run anywhere. The hardest thing I ever had to do was try not to love you when I loved you to my bones.

When I was 8, I had a small fracture in my right arm due to an accident involving a car. My bones have been scared to walk down the street since then.

My nose smells love when I am around you.

My nose has been scared to enter a chemistry lab since the great failed experiment of fuming gas when I was 15.

The hardest thing I ever had to do was try to forget how you smelled, yet with all the forgetfulness I have been given, I still remember.

My eyes, they long for you, yet they have been wise to close themselves since I put shampoo when I was 5.

The hardest thing they ever did was to not look at you while anyone would be insane not to.

My skin drips love like an ocean, but it has been told to stay away from a hot pan since I was 12.

The hardest thing it ever did was not to long your touch. This is how galaxies collide, your skin touching mine.

My heart has been a poet since I was not born.

The first poem it wrote was,

"I wish you were here. I wish things were a little different between us.

I so wish Gods were a little graceful towards us.

All I ever wished was for it to be easy to love you, but fate had a different story written for us."

It had its first heartbreak when I met you, then at 18, then at 22 and then yesterday. I wish my heart had learned stories from my other organs, but my heart has been a poet since I was not born.

- Hands

- You will always be my favorite wish.

- Your memories will always haunt me.

- Like books by the nightstand, the memories whisper at night.

- Like the Dance of Heart by the moon, the wishes find their fight.

The Judge,

The Lawyer,

The Witness,

The God,

Everyone was on your side and so was the Victim.

Tum tuthte tare si ho,
Tut kar bhi khwahishein zaroor puri karti ho.

Ek Lamhe ke shaq se ek khwab tod laya hun.
Ek tere khatir main iss mod pe aaya hun.
Aaj zinda hojaye mohabbat tere bhi dil mein,
Main tere dil ki khatir apna dil tod laya hoon.

You are everything I asked for and yet you are everything I did not ask for.

Words might fall short but I hope you find whatever you are looking for.

I am not sure how many times I have fallen apart but I know that it's more than the times I have fallen asleep.

Jane anjane me tut gaya ek dil se kiya hua wada tha.

Maanlu apni galti, dil ko guroor thoda zyada tha.

Aaj raaste me thokar bhi us pathar se khayi joh humne kal kisi aur pe pheka tha.

Khone ka gum itna hai ki paney ki khushi ab mehsoos nahi hoti.

Woh agar aaj humare paas hote toh unka saath hota, jeb mein unki tasveer nahi hoti.

Humari jami mehfil me aksar naye mehmaan aajate hai.

Vishwas ki unchaiyon pe chadh kar woh aksar wadon se mukar jate hai.

 Na jane kyu dushmani ki adalat me hum aksar apno ko katghare mein khada kartey hai,

Apni barbadi ka ilzam dusron pe lagane se pehley hum aksar khud hi ko saza dete hai.

Tere ghar ke chath se hi chand nikalta hoga,
Kyuki wahi pe humari kayi shame dhali hai.

Kya karogi chand taron ka agar tod bhi laya,

Aao aaj tumhe apne haton se chai banakar pilata hun.

Kya karogi agar duniya se lad bhi gaya tumahre liye,

Chalo shyam ko dono milke khana banate hai.

Zameen aasman ek karne ki batein main nahi karta,

Bartan kapde tum karlena jhaadu pocha mai kardunga.

Taj Mahal kaha se lakar dunga mai aaj ke zamane me,

Apna khud ka ghar lene har maina paise zaroor bachaunga.

Saath samandar paar karke kyu aana chahti ho tum,

Aao nadi kinare dono kuch waqt bitate hai.

Saath janam ke wadon me kyu ulajhna hai,

Kal subah jaldi uthkar dono ko kam pe bhi toh jana hai.

Tuthte taron se kya mangna,

Hum dono hamesha ek dusre ki khwahishein puri karne me toh lage hai.

Please leave a review.

>Instagram Profile: _kunalagarwal2_
>Talk to me!

Show the world your love, it needs all the light you have to give.

My every fabric of being is made of yours, the words I bleed are for you!

I am no one and nothing else if not you!

I am all that your heart is made out of, I am everything that loves you!

When I saw her bleed over my broken heart, while others bled on diamonds and wars,

She became my religion.

I imagine what a God like that could do with all of mankind.

I live inside some poems. Some poems live inside of me.

To the poems I die upon and to all the life it brings out of me!

Samajhdar ho kehkar, zamane ne humse sirf samjautha kiya hai.

So please, run after me.
Run after the only thing I want you to.

I tried to play both of our parts while you were gone. I see pieces of you wherever I go.

But it was never easy to be in your shoes and look at myself the way I wanted you to!

Like you could love me.

I couldn't blame you. I couldn't love myself. How could I expect you to?

I don't know my worth but all I know is, I'm worth more than whatever you think it is.

After me, you will look for me.

In places where you go,

In parks and hotels and museums.

In yourself and in Others.

You will look for the one thing that loved you the most.

Yesterday, I saw a bouquet of roses in the trash.

And no one in the world but only you can understand why that would break my heart.

Tumhari Bikhri zulfein dekhkar dil Bikhar gaya.

Bikhri zulfein toh tum sambhal loge par hum apne dil ka kya karenge?

Woh joh neendo me aati ho tum woh jo lehron me samati ho tum.

Kya ho tum?

Mera ishq ho ya meri aadat?

Mera khwab ho ya meri ibadat?

Agar kismat ne chaha toh phir milenge tab tak khayal rakhna apna,

Shayad sansein tumhari hai par jaan hamari.

Tumse raat raat bhar baat karta hun toh ye neend begani lagti hai,

Tum mere khwabon me aati ho kabhi haqeeqat me bhi aao tumhari yaad bahut aati hai.

In the list of things I like to be on is a list of things she writes what she dreams about.

Log mujhe pyaar me pagal samajhte hai,
Khair hai khuda ki kuch log toh mujhey samjahtey hai.

Mehengi toh fursat hai warna sukoon toh tumhari bahon me do pal me mil jata hai.

Aaj phir kisi chahane wale ne dil dukhaya hai,
Aaj phir marne ko dil chahta hai.

The empty space in my heart was once a haven where she used to stay,

now it's just hell where her memories stay.

To all the nights my lips were savouring the taste of your youth!

To the mornings, I still was hungover on you!

To all the days I couldn't live without you!

To all the glasses that don't get high on you!

To all the poems written because of you!

To all the good days you made even better!

To all the bad days you made not so bad!

The perspective of Sin was sold to us because God had created the prospect of Love.

I knew only how to write, so all I did was write.
Insanely,
Obsessively,
Passionately,
Miserably.
I am sorry,
I wish there were other ways of loving you.

Yesterday, I found happiness in a box.
On the porch, someone left a box of things I lost.

I am not sure which category I come in:
The ones who died laughing or
The ones who lived crying or
The ones that knew nothing.

The day we meet, I hope I have mercy on God because,
He cut my wings and forgot I still had claws.

Dates, they are much kinder when they don't mean anything.

The idea of remembering numbers to show that you love them?

To show you still miss them?

Dates, they hold an intimacy that math cannot justify yet.

She was easy to love.

She made you feel like the top of the world.

She made you feel safe.

She was soft, gentle and kind.

She could bring Rome to the ground.

She could make God beg.

The first thing I learned from home is how to run away from it.

You are the dagger I cut my veins with and get astonished on

how much damage I can take, how much love I can spill.

The warmth of her hugs,
It mocks the Sun.

I sensed that in the misery I lived in,
I began to love everything around me, but me.

Agli baar milne aao toh waqt lekar aana,

Aadhi adhuri mulaqaton se rishtey aadhe adhure reh jate hai.

The mute sky, yet everyone talks to it;
The mute sky, yet it listens to everyone!

Where did she end? Where did I begin?

What am I if not the stardust of her being?

Whatever we both are made out of, isn't it the same fabric?

With the right words,

With the right steps,

With the way not like I loved you,

Would you have loved me back?

If I had loved you in a way that I never learned?

Gehrayi teri ankhon ki aur ghar uss samandar ka,
Nami teri ankhon ki aur pani uss samandar ka,
Namak dono mein tha par aag sirf ek me lagi thi
Samandar jal gaya aur tere aansu dekh mai bikhar gaya.

The only form of control I ever learned is to do it yourself before others do or destroy yourself before others do.

A few came with keys and others with lock picks, but the door to her heart, unwillingly yet often, was opened by axes.

The one who saves the demons,
The one who doesn't run away from them,
The one who teaches them love,
The one who makes the devil turn kind, turn human,
Their love, it must be full of grief and heartache.

I did not let her breathe, like a heavy blanket that kept her warm, that burnt her.

She wanted to throw me off like a broken bulb,

Today, she is wrapped in paper, and she can only think of how I never let her feel the cold.

I know for sure that,

History won't remember me as fondly and beautifully as a lover

But I sincerely hope you do remember me as a poet.

Remember,

You are loved.

Forgive yourself for the battles you have lost.

People don't come alive often out of lost wars.

Unlove.

A myth.

    A tragedy.

        A lie.

A word not invented yet!

How do I punish myself?

It was never justified what I did to myself. No one has been more harsh to me than myself.

They always taught.
The intoxication of any kind is bad;
Drugs,
Cigarettes,
Alcohol.
Then why didn't they ever mention Love?

The storms,

The wars,

The cries,

The beauty.

To hide them all, I close my eyes.

To fall in love,
It's like a war.
One God,
All atrocities
and no peace.

So, choose your words with great care and grace.

The right set of words can heal any person.

The right set of words wield the power to break any person.

Kal milne aana mujhse ek kissa sunaunga

Kaise log barbad hote hai pyaar me bataunga

Tumhare dil ke haal apne lafzon se bayan karunga

Mehsoos kar sako us dard ko woh nazariya samjhaunga

Ek tarfa pyaar kaise karte hai log, tumko bhi sikhaunga

Roshni bharde un andere dilon me woh diya jalaunga

Teri hasi aur mayoosi se apni kavitayen sajaunga

Har roz tere naam ek kagaz kiya, un sabko jodkar ek kitab banaunga

Har kagaz pe ek hi kissa likhta gaya, socha nahi ithna pagal banjaunga

Log kehne lage bhula nahi tujhe toh kissa mai khud banjaunga

Tum kal milne aaja mujhe, mai shayad yahi kissa wapas sunaunga

Woh ek bar mujhse mohabbat karti, bewafa hi sahi mujhe yaad toh karti.

Main ek bar marjata, pagalon sa sahi use pyaar toh karta.

Har roz ye kehna zaruri tha kya? Haq mera jatana zaruri tha kya?

Main teri nahi hoon, ye yaad dilana zaruri tha kya?

On the judgment day
We have a trial with GOD,
Because he's the one on trial!
He needs to justify for all the sins he did to us,
For all the crimes he committed.
And we get to be the judge of it.
He holds no power there.

If you ever need me, I am just one thought away.

Did you ever fall in love?

Did you ever see your love fall in love with someone else?

Did you ever see your love slip from your hands?

Did you ever see your love walking away from you?

Did you see your love fall into some other arms?

These are a few questions that I will ask God the day he deserves to meet me.

I am someone who knows grief and loss,

So,

I will take you to the movies and let your eyes spill all the tears.

I will take you to parks and give you sympathy kisses.

I will take you to museums and compliment the art out of you.

I will take you to all my favorite places and say I love you.

So,

Break in my arms, if you must, for I'll hold you, hold you tight that no pieces threatening to fall apart escapes me.

In the list of things that I love, which starts with the moon and ends with you,

I write my name after you.

Kaash tujhe bhi faraq padta,

Mere hasne se,

Mere rone se,

Mere na hone se.

The thief that stole the smiles of all during the day,

I am sure he still cries by himself into the night, after all.

I am a broken glass with bandages all over it,
I can't hold wine and all I ever asked was for someone to kiss me.

I never want to give you reasons to stay,

I just want you to stay irrespective of anything and everything.

Was it fair?

I gave you a billion reasons to stay and

You gave me only one to leave.

Should I just pick up the pieces and start building it again?

Or the rubble, should I throw at others as hard as I can?

I don't believe in beginnings and endings anymore,

I just know that I was born to love, and I am sick of not having it.

So, I'll bleed if you want me to,

I'll not blame you for asking me to.

But I won't apologize for covering your hands in blood.

Life Imprisonment.

I will tell you all the sins I have committed,
Will you be the judge of it and love me anyway?

Would you love your convicted for the rest of their lives?

In another lifetime, like you wanted, we will just be friends.

In another lifetime, like I wanted, we will be lovers.

But for this lifetime, we are strangers like neither of us wanted.

I am not very touched by all the languages we have created.

So many feelings and only a dictionary to let it all out.

So many words and yet most important things remain unspoken.

Zamane ko naap kar aasman khone aaya hun.

Baarishon ki chath pe khud ka naam likhne aaya hun.

Zameen daav par lagi hai aur khud ko bazar me bechne aaya hoon.

And when you leave a bookmark on this page,

Remember that you will have to pick it up again tomorrow from here,

You will have to pick everything up in life from the very point it made you stop.

I have spent nights looking and searching for poems to be sent to her.

Only to realize that I wrote a book for everyone else to read instead.

How lucky does that make me?

To have something that breaks my heart to say goodbye.

Waqt se churaye huey lamho ka hisaab lene aaya hoon.
In lamho me betaye waqt ka karz utarne aaya hoon.
Tu luta apna waqt gairon pe,
Main tujhse bewaqt milne ki saazish laya hoon.

Kuch logon ka rehna apne saath nahi hota,

Yaadein saath hoti toh hai par saath me unka haath nahi hota.

Shaam dhalne ka intezar uss chand ko bhi hai.

Kuch adhura joh tere andar hai, uss chand mein bhi pura hona baaki hai.

Teri khoobsurati ke bare me kya likhu, uss kitaab ka pura hona abhi baaki hai.

Kismat se milne wale aksar ek dusre ko bhool jate hai.
Ittefaq se milne wale aksar marzi se bichad jate hai.

Woh joh kehar aayi thi zindagi me
Woh ye keh kar chali gayi ki ab bas, ab koi aur chahiye.

Mere ishq ki chhor meri zindagi tabah hai tujhpe,

Woh jo shehar jala diya tha, woh shehar aaj bhi marta hai tujhpe.

If it should come to that point then,

I'll steal you from the world and leave it to rot without you.

Nasha behta hai tumhari ankhon se mujhe nashe me hi rehne do,

Maine maikhaney khali kardiye par mujhe woh nasha mila nahi kisi bhi bottal me.

Main ghar me sabse chota hun, mere hissse me sab kuch aayega.

Jis din batwara hoga tum mere aur baki sab tumhara.

Woh upar wala makaan tumahra aur mai tumahre dil me reh jaunga

Woh badi wali gadi tumahri main nange paun tumahre bataye kadam par chalunga

Tumhari khwahishon ka dhyan rakhunga aur kuch kam padhgaya toh khud ko nilam kardunga

Ye Ramayan toh nahi par mauka mila toh vanvas pe nikal jaunga aur nahi mila toh tumhari chappal leke ghar chala lunga.

Woh khafa toh khud se bhi hua karti hai hume pyaar na karne ke khayal se

Woh bewafa toh nahi par wafa karne ki bhi use aadat nahi

Woh beparwah badi aasani se hojati mere uske pas aane se

Woh roothti bahut jaldi hai mere usko manane ke irade se

Woh ladki bewaqt mila nahi karti aur waqt pe woh hamesha aaya nahi karti

Woh dua me baithi ladki na jane kya maang rahi thi, laal si aankhein, hooton pe thodi pyaas aur kitaab sa chehra ye saaf zaahir kar raha tha woh mere liye khuda se khud ka ek hissa maang rahi thi.

Aaj ek aisi kavita likhu joh sabd likhu woh sach ho jaye

Main waqt likhu tu tham jaye

Main itr likhu tu mehak jaye

Main khwab likhu tu so jaye

Main sharab likhu tu behak jaye

Main aayina likhu tu dikh jaye

Main khoobsurat likhu aur tujhe kuch na ho

Main gunah likhu tujhe pyaar hojaye

Main shaam likhu tu pighal jaye

Main diwana likhu tu hojaye

Main baarish likhu tu baras jaye

Main likhu tera naam kisi kagaz par aur uss kagaz ko bhi tujhse pyaar hojaye.

Maine aksar dekha hai insaan ki mohabbat baanth te huey

Daulat me,

Logon me,

Cheezo me,

Baaton me,

Iradon me,

Khud me,

Khud ke jazbaton me,

Khuda me,

Aur gairon me.

Woh jo likhte hai apno ko kho kar, kya kamal likte hai shabdo ko paakar.

Woh jo likhte hai bewafa kisi ka hokar, kya kamaal likhte hai kisi aur ki wafa par.

Woh jo likhte hai tut kar, kya kamaal likhtey hai bikhrey huey dil par.

Woh jo likhte hai saadgi pe kisi aur ki, koi padhleta hai yaad mein kisi aur ki.

Jahaan khade the hum dono sath mein, ab meri wahan koi jagah nahi.

Jisse shuru hui thi yeh kahani ab woh aagaaz nahi.

Tumne chhoda bhi toh mujhe aise ki ab main kisi aur ke kaabil nahi.

Ek din main tumse puchunga ki tumne mujhse kabhi pyaar kiya tha, tum bhejijak jhoot boldena.

Mushkil waqt me bina kuch soche tum mujhe chhodh dena.

Kisi aur ki baahon me sukoon mile toh hamari wafa ka hisaab kardena.

Kisi aur ke alfaz me khud ke hone ka ehsaas lage, mere sare khat wapas kar dena.

Jis din lage ye kahani puri nahi ho sakti, uss din kitaab ka ye panna badal dena.

I loved her beyond everything, beyond science, beyond the laws of attraction.

I would have to let go of her like gravity has to let go of this universe.

In a world where humans came with User Manuals,

It would have been easy for me to know what made you smile.

I would have known the right set of words that would have made you stay.

We would have shared our manuals and talked about all the troubleshooting techniques.

Mine would have been "The Moon, Letters and A Kiss on the Forehead from You."

I sometimes wonder what would have been yours.

In the little caution segment of your book, it would have been written, "Fragile, handle with love."

I would have read you and your manual over and over like a Bible and then I would have burned it.

In your happy section, there would have been "eat plenty of food, have 12 hours of sleep, laugh, read and travel."

There would have been written that I will never be able to see you in a way where I don't love you.

In the disclaimer section of all our manuals, there would have been written "Important information! Take care of your veins and keep exercising. They are the only organ that runs against gravity, the only organ that runs against all odds."

My user manual would have been in a closet, eating dust with little blood on it. I would have thrown it after I knew how to cut my veins to stop the pain.

All that blood spilt would have had your name written on it.

I wish we all came with user manuals.

Tum chaho ya na chaho,
Tumhari marzi ho ya na ho,
Duniya tumhe bhagna sikha degi,
Tumhe baithna sikhna padega.

Use mujhe chup karana aata tha,
Use mujhe manana aata tha,
Uske pyaar ko khatm hote huey maine dekha hai,
Maine kal rat use kisi aur ko manate dekha tha.

Very few understood my poem and fewer understood the silence in between lines of my poems.

Bataon main kaise use bewafa kahu?
Maine toh uski bewafai se bhi mohabbat ki hai.

I want to come home to you.

I want to see your beautiful face every day.

I want to kiss your forehead a thousand times.

I want us to make breakfast together.

I want us to fight.

I want us to love each other irrationally.

I want us to get married.

I want us to have kids.

I want to argue over what we are going to name them.

I want us to buy a house with our names on the plate.

I want us to go around the world.

I want us to get a dog and a cat.

I want us to grow old together, live together and die together.

This is all I want.

God tell me, is it too much to ask?

My body is a fleabag and the heart is a room with the number 401.

The room has always been known for its horrendous appearance, cookies crumbled, books unorganized and torn, broken whiskey glasses, blood splatter, damp walls, oxidized paint and dying plants.

People have visited room 401 less often than not, but of those who did visit the room, some were just passers-by, astonished by its horrid they never entered it.

Few have tried to enter it but left just as glass pierced their leg or the dampness scared them. There were some who tried to clean it up but just gave up too soon, but there was this one girl. She visited room 401 as if it was her home. She made a picture of how beautiful it could be, she entered the room and put her fragrance all over it, she lit scented candles in the room, she touched the books with her warm and kind hands and put them on a bookshelf. She took all the glass shatters and threw them out and in the process, she hurt herself too, but that did not let her down. She vacuumed the place, she painted the walls peach with love, she kissed those plants and watered them.

She put a picture of herself on the fridge. It was beautiful to look at.

Soon, there came news that there was a new fleabag in town. She left as soon as she heard that.

Someone, please come and put it the way it was before she visited. Please, I liked it better that way.

The new room does not belong to me.

What would you do if you found death was in love with you?

Death is a Pariah. It's a lady in a red scarf and a jumpsuit. Death comes to you as all the things you have never experienced, it comes to you as all the pain you have never endured, and it comes to you as all the love you have never felt. It walks on to you one morning in a coffee shop or for a night walk and says, "I'm death, but you still have time." It says it wants to fall in love with you before it takes you away.

And when she says love, you multiply it with infinity and take it to the depths of eternity and you will still have barely a glimpse of what she's talking about.

It stalks you every day and leaves you flowers and ice cream on the porch.

She gives you memories of being old together and sooner or later death becomes close to you.

One fine day, death sits on a bench in a park with a dagger in its chest. It bleeds and bleeds and bleeds all the love you ever gave her and what you can all see is grief all over the red love.

You ask, "It's hard to let go of me?"

She says, "Yes, it is."

You reply, "Please let me be the one losing."

Death grins and tricks you into taking your life.

What would you do if you ever found that death is in love with you and you with it?

Sonchta hun…

Koi humare liye bhi dua mangta hoga?

Koi humare liye bhi raat raat bhar jaagta hoga?

Ey zindagi ye kaisa khel hai,

Iss chakravyuh ke toh sare Abhimanyu hai.

Uske saath har subah chai peene ke khayal me
Humne raat raat bhar sharab ko chum rakha tha.

Itna gum hai ki khud se chupna chahata hun.
Tum wahi dekhte ho joh main dikhana chahata hun

Aap baaton ki baat kartey ho woh humse khamoshi me rooth jati thi.

Agar humare hisse me khamoshi aayi hai toh koi humsafar hai uska jiske hisse mein awaaz aayi hogi.

Main dushman hi sahi mujhe awaaz de mohabbat se,

Main raqeeb se bhi dosti karlunga tu naam toh le mera ek baar pyaar se.

Maine apni har mohabbat se ek aadat sikhi hai.

Maine sikha toot jana apni pehli mohabbat me.

Maine sikha sharab peena apni dusri mohabbat se.

Maine sikha bikhar jaana uske badh wali mohabbat me.

Maine sikha daga karna aaj wali mohabbat se.

Maine sikha bhul jana kal wali mohabbat se.

Maine sikha wafa karna kabhi na aane wali mohabbat se.

I believe in God, that's because I have seen her whisper into his ear, but what is God to her love anyway?

I believe in the devils and the demons, that's because the greatest trick she ever managed to pull off was convincing the devil that he was in love with her and the boundaries a devil would cross for love are unfathomable.

Raasten bhatak kar yu tere karib aaya hun

Taaron ko samjha kar unhe tere paas laya hun

Agar hai koi naam dusra pyaar ka toh tere naam ko main usse badal ne aaya hu.

One day, you will leave and never miss me.

You will not miss me; you'll rather miss the feeling of being divine.

You will miss the way you made me laugh, like a morale that gave you a purpose to stay. To stay because you matter.

You will miss the way I made you laugh, like you wanted to stay a little more for yourself. To forget that the air you have been breathing chokes a little.

You will miss the way you shattered me all over the place like every piece glittered stardust out of it. You will miss the awe in your eyes seeing something so broken and yet something so beautiful.

You will miss the way I made you angry just to soothe you later like dusk had faded only for dawn to occur.

You will miss the way we held our hands together like our souls were burning on fire.

You will miss my writings, the way I described you, the way I made you feel like you would want to read more about yourself, and I would like to write more about you.

You will not miss me; my writings will haunt you more than my memories.

You will not miss me; you will miss the part of yourself that you gave me.

Aaj ek khat maine tere naam ka phir jalaya hai

Main padh na saku alfaaz tere aisa tune bhi toh apni nigahon ko chupaya hai.

I won't ask you where or whether it hurts.

I will just kiss all over the place and you wouldn't remember if it even hurts in the first place.

Tum chahoge mujhe mere chale jane ke baad

Tum barbaad hojayogey mere mukar jane ke baad.

Woh jo saadgi sajti thi tumhare chehre pe, tum hasna bhul jaogey mere ruth jane ke baad.

Wo bagicha joh sirf phoolon se khil raha tha,
Na jane kyu wo sukhey patoh ko bhul raha tha.

And by the time love knocked on my door, I was already in bed with my hatred for it.

I'll meet you one day all alone in the ether. We'll talk about that day we met. We'll see the clear sky by the river, count the stars and you won't be in a hurry to leave. I'll get you your favourite flowers and read you all the lines from the book.

In another lifetime, we'll meet at the right time and at the right place and it'll all be alright.

The last time Cupid Angles shot someone,
Love held my right hand and poetry held my left hand.

I don't know if it's the tragedy of pain or the mercy of it,

I cannot feel yours, and you cannot understand mine.

Sometimes, I read about you to my poems.

Suno, main tumhare upar ek kitaab likhunga. Ek panne pe tumhari adah, dusre pe tumhari wafa likhunga. Gulab se mehkenge har ek alfaaz, padhne wala bhi mehsoos karega har ek jazbaat. Kalam se nikli syahi aur dil se nikla pyaar dono khoob bharunga. Uss kitaab ko main apne dil ke paas hi rakhunga.

Suno, main tumhare upar ek kitaab likhunga. Ek panne pe teri buraiyan likhunga, uss khuda se naraz main uski hi khamiya likhunga. Khud ka ek kirdar likh kar tujhe khuda ka hi darja dunga. Padhne wala dua bhi padega aur tere aankhon me dabi har gehrayi ko bhi samjhega.

Uss kitaab me kaid tu logon ki ibadat banegi, teri bandish hi unki bandagi hogi aur iss pyaar ke dharam pe main tera hi naam likhunga. Kyu apna milna ittefaq tha ye sawaal likhunga aur kyu apna bichadna naseeb hai iska jawab bhi dhundunga. Iss kaarigari se main pyaar ka ek naya arth likhunga. Aasman aur zameen ko sath likh kar tere mere faasle hi khatm kar dunga. Labon pe tere jo tehri thi meri kami, main us kami ko pura karunga. Tu bane na khwab har ek ka aisi teri muqammal dastan main uss kitaab me likhunga.

Suno, mai tumhare upar ek kitaab likhunga. Chand bhi tujhse sharma jaye aisi teri kahani likhunga. Teri zulfon ko meri zameen maan kar main ek itihaas likhunga. Mere khwabon ki razai me tere saath saath main apni zindagi likhunga. Ab aur kya kya likhunga, ye kitaab ka aakhri panna hai iss kitaab ka naam main "***Mohabatt, Khat aur Tum***" likhunga.

Yes, this might be the end!
Of the Story.
Of the Poem.
Of the Book.
But, also the beginning of our journey together!

A letter to the reader.

Hope this finds you in good health and full of love. The book and this letter have travelled miles to reach you because no one gets to get you so easily. I genuinely hope that this book deserves to be read by you.

You and I, we are all stories; by now, you probably know me better than I know you, but if you think about it, I do know you in ways that no one knows. I know there must be a terrible distance between us, but we all look at the same sky. We all are bound towards one fate like the most beautiful collision ever.

There are many things in life, so subtle yet so beautiful that they hurt, like all things about the universe and you. We all are afraid to admit things we want the most and that is what makes us human. Isn't it crazy how we humans are just meant to hold each other? The whole of the universe is unimaginable, but I'm not sure why it fits just right in our hands, fits just right in our arms.

From the beginning of time, we were designed innately to love, so be the light that the dark world is looking out for. You are the star it needs; don't let anything in life turn you bitter; let it turn you gentle, humble and importantly kind. Kind towards people and kind towards yourself.

So go out there, love extraordinarily, love your heart out and get broken if it needs you to. Only the love full of heartache and grief is something worth breaking for. You are worth breaking for. There resides a universe within you. Like roots and like the branches of a tree, you are complete. It's the balance we hold onto. The good and evil are all within us.

Beautiful people aren't just found anywhere. The most beautiful people I have met are those who make good friends with grief, heartache, loss and struggle. This is what makes them sensitive to things around them. They are full of kindness, love and genuine concern towards humanity.

But I hope you find someone to love you when you are not so lovable, don't have poems to share, run out of stories to tell, and are vulnerable. I wish from the bottom of my heart that they will love you irrespective of anything and everything in the world. If you have to take anything away from this book or as a personal piece of advice, I would like to say that never become a reason for someone to give up on love and all the other good things in the world.

As you reach the last page of this book, Goodbyes are in order. This book has been a very close part of me and, hopefully, now to you, and all the words are just what we feel.

The things you read are not with lips but with eyes. The comforting things are those read by the heart, felt by the bones and shown by the tears.

About the Author

Kunal Agarwal

Born in Hyderabad and in the wrong generation, the writer of "Mohabbat, Khat and you" is a hopeless romantic who searches for solace in words weaved with passion and feelings, He tries to look at the world as a place full of love. He knows that the world holds unbelievable joy and wonder but also it is full of sadness and loss. He is not just an individual but a collective of experiences, he is all those people who have loved him and also those who did not. The author loves cats and dogs. He is a traveller and loves to visit new places. He loves to meet and talk to new people about their stories and perspectives on vivid things that make up the universe, about love and almost every other thing.

www.ingramcontent.com/pod-product-compliance
Lightning Source LLC
LaVergne TN
LVHW041943070526
838199LV00051BA/2891